MAKE it WORK!

ARCTIC
PEOPLES

Andrew Haslam & Alexandra Parsons

TWO-CAN
in association with
WATTS BOOKS

First published in Great Britain in 1995 by
Two-Can Publishing Ltd
346 Old Street
London EC1V 9NQ
in association with
Watts Books
96 Leonard Street
London EC2A 4RH

A catalogue record for this book is available from the British Library.

Hardback ISBN: 1 85434 274 6
Paperback ISBN: 1 85434 275 4

Managing Editor: Christine Morley
Editor: Jacqueline McCann
Designer: Helen McDonagh
Art Director: Jill Plank
Deputy Art Director: Carole Orbell
Picture Researcher: Sam Riley
Model-makers: Paul Holzherr, Melanie Williams

Thanks also to: Colin and Jenny at Plough Studios.

Models: Anton Ajetunmobi, Daniel Bradford, Vanisha Cozier, Tendai Dhliwayo, James Hensby, Zakiyyah Hussain,
Emily McClymont, Michael Manatsa, CJ Marshall, Lynette Marshall, Thomas O'Brian, Emma Sainsbury, Anna Smith

Photographic credits:
Arthur Phillips: p9, p59 (maps); Bryan & Cherry Alexander: p5 (tl, br), p 12 (tr), p20, p29, p36, p37, p40, p42, p44, p46, p48 (bl),
p60 (ml, br), p61; British Museum: p30, p34 (tr), p60 (tr); Canadian Museum of Civilization: p4 (no. 39638), p32 (bl, no. 51166);
Derek Fordham: p5 (bl); Magnum: F Mayer, p23, p32 (tl); McCord Museum of Canadian History, Notman Photographic Archives:
p28 (no. MP595(2)), p38, (no. MP1971(9)), p48 (tr, no. MP597(186)); National Archives of Canada: p31 (no. PA110844), p47
(no. PA114667); Range/Bettmann: p45, p50, p58 (2); Werner Forman Archive: p12 (br), p35, p56.

All other photographs by Jon Barnes
Printed and bound by G. Canale & C. SpA, Turin, Italy

Hardback 2 4 6 8 10 9 7 5 3 1
Paperback 2 4 6 8 10 9 7 5 3 1

Contents

Studying arctic life

△ The Eskimos lived almost entirely off the animals they hunted, eating the meat and using the hides to make clothing and homes. This woman is chewing a piece of sealskin, which makes it softer and easier to work with.

All human beings need food and shelter to survive. Many also have a system of beliefs that gives shape and meaning to their lives. Throughout history, people have created different ways of meeting these basic requirements. By studying the peoples of the **Arctic** and **subarctic** we learn how they used the resources around them to build shelters and find food, and how they developed a way of life that sustained them.

IN THIS BOOK we will look at how arctic peoples lived about 200 years ago, before their lives were changed by the arrival of Europeans and Americans. We can build up a picture of the Eskimo way of life from the stories told by present-day arctic peoples, writings of early explorers and traders, and the studies of **anthropologists** and **archaeologists**. In this way we can begin to understand Eskimo culture.

◁ Eskimos fished and hunted land and sea mammals in all weather conditions.

THE ARCTIC is the most northerly region of the world. It is a vast wilderness of mountains, **tundra** and ice. The subarctic is the area directly south of the Arctic Circle, below the **tree line**. Despite the enormous size of the Arctic and subarctic, the peoples who lived and continue to live there found similar solutions to the problems they faced. We have used the following divisions, where necessary, to introduce information that relates more to one group than another (see page 7).

KEY FOR SYMBOLS

(snowhouse)   **eastern Arctic**

(bowhead whale)   **western Arctic**

(snow-shoe)   **subarctic**

THE STORY OF ARCTIC SETTLEMENT is really the story of how people developed the skills necessary to exploit a very cold and inhospitable climate. The Arctic is rich in terms of food resources, but the demands of day-to-day life were such that people had to be extremely tough, both physically and mentally, to survive.

COMMON TO ALL PEOPLES OF THE ARCTIC was the belief that the world around them and all things in it had both a practical and sacred aspect. Their world was dominated by many spirits. Everything, from mountains to stones or **artefacts**, was believed to possess a spirit, just as animals and people did. It is important to remember that everything in the Eskimo's world had a deep religious significance.

THE WORD 'ESKIMO' has been used for many years by Europeans and Americans to refer to arctic peoples, although it is not an arctic word. It is thought to be an Ojibwa Indian word meaning 'raw meat eaters', or a Montagnais word meaning 'snow-shoes'. In general, arctic peoples such as **Inuits** and **Yupiks**, referred themselves with words that mean 'real human beings'. However, as there is no single word that covers all the different groups of people living in the Arctic and subarctic, we shall use Eskimo.

◁ *The winter camp of Siberian caribou herders.*

THE MAKE IT WORK! way of looking at history is to ask questions of the past and find some of the answers by making replicas of the things people made. However, you do not have to make everything in the book to understand the arctic peoples' way of life. Some of the objects included are based on sacred or ceremonial traditions and therefore should be treated with respect.

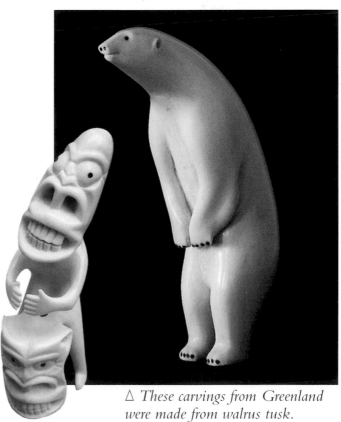

△ *These carvings from Greenland were made from walrus tusk.*

A harsh, icy haven

Thousands of years ago, during the **Ice Age**, the ice cap at the top of the world was a great deal larger than it is today. The climate was also considerably colder and the sea level much lower. What are now shallow seas were then dry land, and Siberia, Alaska, northern Canada, the Aleutian islands and Greenland were all linked together.

▷ *This is a relief map of the arctic region.*

BIG GAME HUNTERS headed northwards during the Ice Age. They came in large groups from the empty plains of northern Asia and Siberia, following herds of mammoth and other animals. They crossed the Bering Sea land bridge and spread outwards from Alaska to as far away as Greenland. Later, the ice cap melted and sea covered the land between Siberia and Alaska, making it difficult to return.

IN THE NORTH the hunters found an icy wilderness, where the soil could not be cultivated and few trees grew. But they also found plentiful supplies of fresh water and abundant wildlife: whales, walrus, seals, **caribou** (known as reindeer in Europe), birds and musk ox. Over many centuries, people adapted to a life of snow, ice and chilling winds.

▽ *Indigenous vegetation.*

moss

berries

fir tree (tree line)

▷ *Indigenous wildlife.*

polar bear
caribou
wolf
reindeer
arctic fox

walrus
seal
whale
salmon
arctic char

ptarmigan
guillemot
nesting birds

THE EASTERN ARCTIC refers to the polar regions of Greenland and eastern Canada.

Eastern Arctic peoples:

Greenland: *Inuit*
E. Canada: *Inuit, Netsilik*

THE WESTERN ARCTIC refers to the polar regions of North America, western Canada and the Aleutian Islands.

Western Arctic peoples:

Western Canada: *Copper Inuit*
Aleutian Islands: **Aleut**
Alaska: *Inuit, Yupik*

THE SUBARCTIC is the area south of the Arctic Circle. It covers the north of the American continent, the top of the Asian landmass and the most northerly areas of Europe.

Subarctic peoples:

N. American Indians: *Cree, Kutchin*
Eurasians: *Chukchi, Yakuty, Nentsy Eveny, Evenki*
Europeans: *Saami (Lapps)*

The arctic climate

The Arctic is actually a desert made up almost completely of ice. As it hardly ever rains, there is very little snow. Temperatures are well below zero for most of the year, and freezing winds whip across the landscape. However, during the short summer, the sun shines for much of the day and the ice melts to reveal scrubland.

SPRING in the Arctic usually begins during March. It is still cold, but the days are getting longer and the sun begins to shine. Seals come out of the sea to bask in the sun, so the Eskimos would move on to the ice to hunt the seals, before the ice became too thin to walk on. As the temperature rises, the ice begins to thaw and break up and the hunters leave the ice floe to live on the land.

▽ *The Arctic in summer: temperatures rise and the ice recedes. Eskimos move to new hunting grounds.*

portable summer dwelling

permafrost *stops trees and shrubs taking root*

hunters move to the tundra in summer

THE SUN SHINES for at least part of the day from March to September and temperatures in some inland regions can rise to 16° centigrade. The sun melts the ice and snow covering the land, but it does not reach the **permafrost**, a permanently frozen layer of soil under the surface.

DURING SUMMER, mosses, grasses, lichens and low shrubs grow on the vast swampy plain, or tundra, that extends from the polar ice cap in the north, to the tree line in the south. The Eskimos would travel inland to hunt the huge caribou herds that came to graze on the tundra.

▷ *Men travel to the edge of the **ice floe.** They hunt for seals and fish for tom-cod and char through **breathing holes.***

hunters build temporary homes

A WHITEOUT is a deadly arctic hazard. It happens mainly on cloudy summer days when light seems to come from all around, casting no shadows. It is impossible to tell left from right, or north from south. The only thing to do is sit still and wait for the light to change.

▽ In summer the earth tilts towards the sun.

Sun ▽

▽ In winter the earth tilts away from the sun.

◁ The earth spins around the sun, turning on its own axis. In the first half of the year the earth tilts towards the sun; in the second half it tilts away – this is why we have seasons.

ARCTIC SEASONS are very distinct from one another. In summer, the sun rarely sinks below the horizon and there is almost continual daylight. In winter, the sun's rays are at such a low angle that they hardly rise above the horizon. It is almost permanently dark.

◁ In late spring and summer Eskimos hunt in coastal areas from their **kayaks**.

BY EARLY WINTER, the ice has frozen to around three metres deep and is safe to walk on. The lack of daylight makes hunting difficult, but it is possible to fish through holes cut in the ice. Eskimos also hunted in areas of open sea, called **polynyas**, which never freeze over due to strong currents.

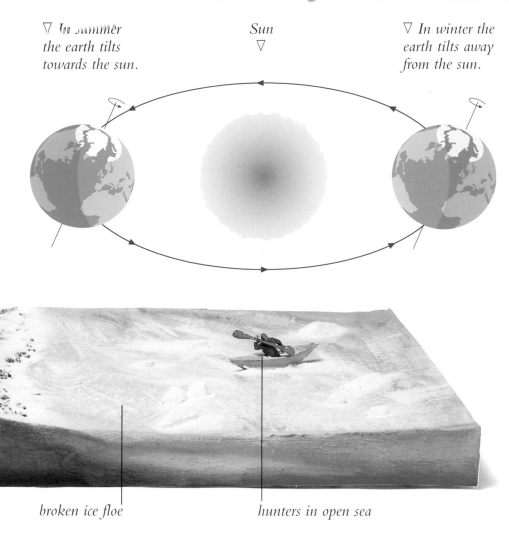

broken ice floe   hunters in open sea

IN AUTUMN, temperatures begin to fall and the caribou start to migrate south. When **freeze-up** begins, the sea ices over, preventing boat travel. While the ice is soft, it is also dangerous walk on. During this time, the Eskimos would hunt the last of the caribou and perhaps dig a new **sod house**.

▽ The Arctic in winter – temperatures drop and Eskimos move on to the ice to hunt sea mammals.

huskies pulling sleds

Keeping warm – staying alive

Keeping warm was a matter of life and death in the Arctic, and clothes were the Eskimo's main defence against the cold. Animal skins were sewn together very carefully with animal **sinews** to make warm clothing. Arctic peoples had very distinctive ways of decorating their clothes, using feathers, bones, or bird quills, not only as decorations, but also as **amulets**. Above all, they thanked the spirit of the animal that clothed them.

EACH GROUP OF PEOPLE developed its own characteristic look which was reflected in its costumes. This meant that strangers approaching a settlement could be recognized from a safe distance simply by their outline.

PEOPLE OF THE SUBARCTIC were spread out over a wide area. In Siberia and other parts of Eurasia, caribou skins were often used to make clothes, while North American Indians also used moose hides. Common to all groups was the use of the snow-shoe. In winter, these tennis-racquet-shaped, strap-on soles made it easier to cross drifts of soft snow without sinking.

snow-shoes

caribou-skin tunic

harpoon

caribou-skin tunic

loose, all-in-one caribou suits worn by mother and baby

subarctic Indian hunter

Chukchi woman from Siberia

Inuit hunter from Canadian eastern Arcti

WESTERN ARCTIC MEN, such as the Yupik, wore **labrets** - decorated plugs of ivory or bone, pushed into holes cut on either side of the mouth. These holes were cut during a boy's teenage years. He was expected to show no signs of pain during the ceremony. A man with labrets was seen to be ready for hunting, responsibility and marriage.

WESTERN ARCTIC WOMEN took advantage of Alaska's rich supply of fur-bearing animals, such as ground squirrel, wolf and mink, to make highly decorated costumes. They wore jewellery in the form of earrings and strings of beads, and were tattooed in their teens (see page 53).

EASTERN ARCTIC PEOPLES depended on large sea mammals such as the seal, walrus and whale. By necessity their clothing had to be waterproof as they spent so much time hunting on the ice. In the polar regions, warm leg coverings made from polar bear skins were worn.

WATERPROOF CLOTHING was needed for fishing trips. It was either made of sealskin or strips of sea mammal intestine sewn tightly together. Bird skin clothing was also light, waterproof, durable and warm. These were important alternatives for clothing in the eastern Arctic, where caribou were not common.

finger masks

plain, loose-fitting parka

long caribou-skin parka with rounded flap at front

Inuit woman from Alaska

eastern Arctic, Iglulik **shaman**

eastern Arctic child

THE CARIBOU PARKA is the most effective cold-weather clothing ever invented. It was made of a single layer of loose-fitting fur that was easy to move around in, and worked by trapping the body heat of the wearer. In winter, when temperatures were extreme, double layers were worn for extra insulation.

▷ *These present-day children of the eastern Arctic are wearing parkas made from caribou fur.*

MAKE A WATERPROOF KAMLEIKA

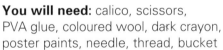

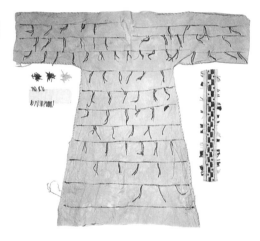

You will need: calico, scissors, PVA glue, coloured wool, dark crayon, poster paints, needle, thread, bucket

1 Lie down on a double layer of calico and ask someone to draw around you in the shape of a smock, as shown above. Cut out the smock shape carefully, making a V shape in the front only for the neck.

2 Measure and cut the cuffs, hem and neck bands, preparing 2 strips for each, about 9 cm wide, as above left.

3 In a bucket, make up a solution of 1 part PVA glue to every 10 parts water. Add light-brown paint. Dip the calico pieces in the solution and scrunch up. Make sure the material is covered. Wring gently and hang up to dry.

4 Use a dark crayon to draw lines across the smock. Paint one of each pair of strips with a simple brown and red pattern as shown above left.

5 Sew along the side seams and across the top of the sleeves. Cut short lengths of coloured wool. Glue them to the back of the cuffs, hem and neck strips as above.

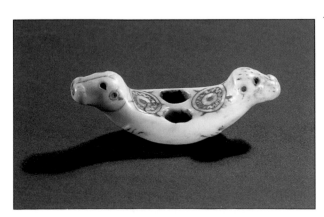

INSIDE OUT OR OUTSIDE IN? If the parka was made of just one layer of skin, the fur side faced inwards and the skin side faced outwards. Often in the winter, two layers were used. The layer nearest the skin had the fur side inside, and the second layer had the fur side outside. The best trim to use for the hood was either wolf or dog fur as breath does not freeze on it.

◁ *This is an ivory belt fastener in the shape of two seals, worn by the Inuit of Alaska.*

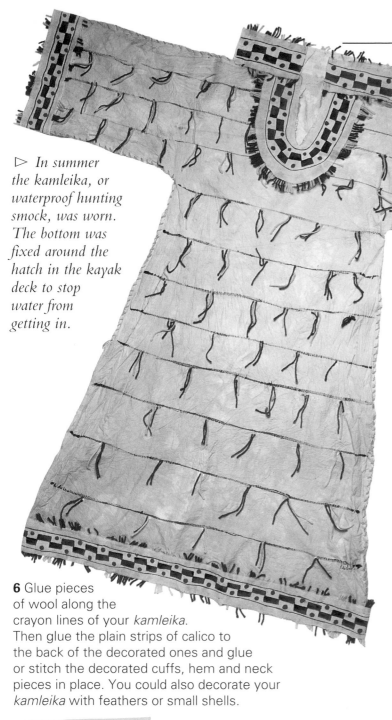

▷ *In summer the kamleika, or waterproof hunting smock, was worn. The bottom was fixed around the hatch in the kayak deck to stop water from getting in.*

ANIMAL HIDES were used to make different types of clothing. Winter parkas were usually made of warm caribou hide, whereas summer parkas were made of lighter, waterproof sealskin. Mothers wore a parka called an *amautik*, which was big enough to tuck a baby in the back and loose enough to swivel the baby around for feeding. Men and women's clothing tended to look very similar. The main differences were in the way that parkas were decorated.

PREPARING SKINS for clothing and tents was the responsibility of the women. Caribou were hunted at the end of summer when their fur had thickened up for winter. Their skins were preferred for clothing because the hairs are hollow and trap more warm air than other furs. The hides had to be scraped clean and dried. Finally, they were chewed or sometimes soaked in urine to soften them.

6 Glue pieces of wool along the crayon lines of your *kamleika*. Then glue the plain strips of calico to the back of the decorated ones and glue or stitch the decorated cuffs, hem and neck pieces in place. You could also decorate your *kamleika* with feathers or small shells.

🐋 MAKE SUMMER HUNTING TROUSERS

You will need: calico, PVA glue and paint mixture as for *kamleika*, dark crayon, needle and thread, string, safety pin

1 Cut out trousers on a double thickness of calico as shown left, using the wearer as a guide for measurements.

2 Make up paint solution as for *kamleika* and dip in the pieces. Leave to dry. Use the crayon to draw on horizontal lines.

3 Sew up the seams. Now turn over the waistband and sew hem for drawstring. Thread string through with a safety pin.

GETTING WET could be fatal in the Arctic. If a hunter fell through the ice while seal hunting, he would have to scramble ashore quickly and roll in soft snow. The snow would act as a sponge, drawing out the water from the clothing. Then, if his inner layer of clothing was not wet and the settlement was close by, the hunter stood a chance of surviving.

WOODEN VISORS AND BONE GOGGLES were worn to protect the eyes, as bright sun reflecting off snow can cause blindness. Visors shaped like base-ball caps, or goggles with narrow slits, helped to reduce the glare.

MAKE AN ALEUT VISOR

You will need: thin card, pencil, glue, calico, scissors, poster paints, thin twigs, beads, string

1 Cut a visor shape from a piece of card about 36 cm square. Cut the same shape from the calico, 2 cm bigger. Glue calico to card, folding edges under, then fold the card into a visor shape.

2 Paint a symmetrical design on the calico. Cut out shapes from card as shown above left and paint. Thread beads on twigs. Glue sticks and shapes to visor. Make 2 holes on each side. Push string through and tie under chin.

KEEPING CLOTHES DRY was of vital importance. When travelling long distances the Eskimos moved at a steady pace to avoid perspiring which might make their parkas damp. If beads of sweat formed they could turn to painful crusts of ice, and possibly lead to frostbite.

BOOTS, or *mukluks,* as they were known in Alaska, were made of waterproof sealskin and worn in summer. Winter boots were made of warmer caribou or occasionally dog fur. The Yupik made socks woven from sea grass to line their boots. They helped to absorb any moisture.

MAKE A PAIR OF MUKLUKS

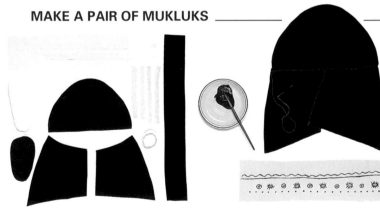

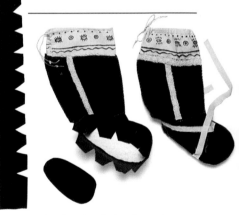

You will need: thick polystyrene tile, craft knife, scissors, velvet or similar fabric, calico, needle and thread, PVA glue, strips of fur-like fabric, paint, string

1 Put your feet on polystyrene and draw around them. Ask an adult to help you cut out the sole shapes.

2 Cut out the shapes and strips, as shown above left, from the velvet (dark), the calico (white) and the fur-like fabric.

3 Sew the two leg pieces to the toe piece as shown above. Then paint the calico top piece with a brown pattern as shown above.

4 Sew up the back of the leg pieces and stitch on the painted calico strip. Glue polystyrene sole into position. Cut notches into the velvet strip and glue around foot piece, folding the notches under the sole. Glue on velvet sole. Seam the calico top and thread string through. Sew calico strips to foot and tie around ankle.

wooden sun visor decorated with sea-lion whiskers – the mark of a skilled hunter

parka hood trimmed with wolf fur

sealskin parka with the fur turned towards the inside

mittens made of sealskin fur or bird skin

trousers worn for warmth by both men and women

summer boots made of sealskin and trimmed with wolf or polar bear fur

DANCING MITTENS were worn by some Eskimo men on ceremonial occasions. These sealskin mitts had puffin beaks sewn all over, which rattled as the men shook the gloves in time to the beat of the drum.

MAKE DANCING MITTENS

You will need: needle and thread, paint, self-hardening modelling clay, calico, scissors, PVA glue

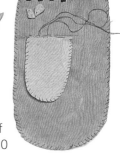

1 Measure around your hand and cut 4 mitten and 4 thumb shapes from the calico.

2 Make a mixture of 1 part PVA glue to 10 parts water. Add yellow-brown paint and dip the calico pieces in the mixture. Soak, then leave to dry.

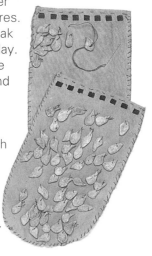

3 Paint a border of brown squares. Make small beak shapes from clay. Pierce a needle hole in each and leave to dry.

4 Cut a slit in one side of each mitten. Insert thumbs and sew as above. Now sew on all of the beaks.

Shelter from cold and wind

Eskimos lived in small, isolated camps, usually consisting of between 10 and 50 people living in up to six dwellings. Everyone came from one extended family that would include uncles, aunts, cousins and in-laws. Eskimos built both temporary and semi-permanent homes for protection against the cold. But their homes were also important meeting places where people gathered to sing and dance, mend weapons, treat hides and celebrate yearly festivals.

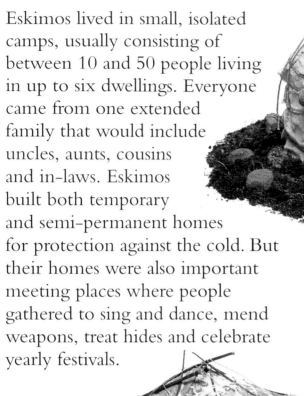

IN SOUTHERN SIBERIA some people lived all year round in cone-shaped, circular tents called **yurts** (see page 23).

IN NORTHERN SIBERIA, the Evenki used caribou skins to cover their portable, beehive-shaped yurts.

THE YAKUTY of eastern Siberia lived in winter dwellings known as cornered log yurts. These were made of logs and roofed with twigs and sods of earth. In summer, they switched to yurts made of birch bark.

THE CREE INDIANS of the North American subarctic built domed winter houses covered with softened caribou hides. The houses were light and strong and could be packed up and transported on a **toboggan**. Inside, the floor was lined with soft, springy, spruce boughs. In summer, they sometimes replaced the skins with sheets of birch bark.

SNOWHOUSES, or *iglu vigas* were used as temporary winter huts by most arctic peoples (see page 20). They were built on frozen sea ice as hunting bases, or for short-term protection against the cold. The Inuit of eastern Arctic lived in them all winter, building a cluster of *iglus* with connecting passageways.

THE SOD HOUSE was the most common winter dwelling (see page 18). Foundations were dug deep into the earth to form a warm living area. The roof, which rose above the ground, was covered with an insulating layer of sod, or turf. In some large Alaskan communities, men gathered in communal sod houses called *kashims* to mend weapons, talk, play games and dance.

BAFFIN ISLANDERS' summer tents had a ridgepole along the top and were rounded at the back. The frames were made of driftwood or arched whale ribs covered with sealskin. Windows were made of bleached sealskin, which was thin enough to let in light. Inside, moss was used to line the tents for extra warmth.

ARCTIC PEOPLES from south Alaska to Quebec in eastern Canada made a summer tent, called a *tupiq*, of sealskin with the fur removed. Poles were made from pieces of driftwood, if it was available, or whalebone. The skin covers were kept in place by heavy stones placed around the base.

ARCTIC PEOPLES were always on the move, from summer camps to winter camps, hunting animals. As a result, their homes had to be either light and portable, or fast to build, using materials that were readily available. During the winter, some Eskimos lived in sod houses. Dug deep beneath the earth for warmth and insulation, they were like huge underground caves. A sod house could also be reused the following winter, if it had not been too badly damaged during the year. Although an ideal winter home, the sod house was too damp and warm for summer.

MEN STARTED WORK ON THE SOD HOUSE when the surface soil had thawed. A wide hole, one or two metres in depth, was dug into the earth to form a communal living area. The entrance was very small, so that the heat from inside could not escape. Some houses were built for one family, while others were up to 20 metres long and home to extended families. At the top of the sod house the air was warmer, so people slept on raised platforms. In some of the larger houses, these were shared by up to 50 people.

MAKE A SOD HOUSE

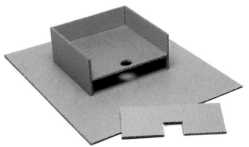

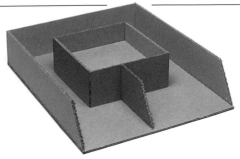

You will need: wooden fruit box, cardboard, short twigs, scraps of sacking, moss (from a florist), glue, craft knife, cutting mat, scraps of fur fabric

1 Cut the base, four walls (one with a door) and floor (with a round hole) as shown above left. Glue together. Cut and glue the side of the entrance tunnel and the outer walls into place.

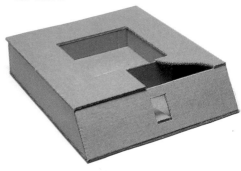

2 Cut and fit sections to cover the ground level. Cut entrance door on 3 sides and fold along bottom to form tunnel. Cut out section to view.

3 Ask an adult to cut wood strips from the fruit box. Glue these to the walls and floor. Build roof frame and sleeping platform with sticks.

4 Add fur scraps for bedding. Leaving a viewing hole in the top, cover the frame with sacking and moss to give an earthy appearance.

IN PARTS OF NORTHERN ALASKA, people lived in permanent whaling communities. Sod houses were lived in all year round. The houses and their occupants were given names such as 'The people with lots of mice', or 'All wet around it', and 'The people who face the sun'.

SEAL-OIL LAMPS usually belonged to the wife in a family group. In the evening, a woman would light the moss wick and place her lamp on the raised platform. The heat that was generated by the slow-burning lamp and the body heat of the people inside, kept everyone warm.

a gap in the roof lets in light (sometimes transparent sea-mammal intestine is used as a window pane)

THE ENTRANCE TO A SOD HOUSE was via an underground passage that also served as a storage and cooking area. Before entering the sod house, an Eskimo would use an *anautaq*, or snow-beater, to brush the snow off his or her outer garments. Then he would take off his mittens, boots and parka and hang them up to dry over a seal-oil lamp.

single platform for sleeping on

framework of whalebone or wood, covered with sods of earth and sealskin

chambers for storing food and drying clothes

△ *This Inuit hunter has almost completed his snowhouse – all he needs to do now is to build an entrance tunnel.*

IN THE WINTER SEASON, snow was the only building material available on the ice floe, so the Inuit learned how to use it to make temporary homes. Snow is made up of flakes of ice and pockets of air and is an excellent insulation material.

THE WORD 'IGLU' actually means 'home' and can apply to any kind of dwelling. The dome-shaped snowhouse, which we know as an 'igloo', is called an *iglu-viga* (snowhouse) in the Inuit language.

BUILDING AN IGLU required many years of practice. If necessary, a skilled hunter could build an *iglu* in an hour, even in the pitch dark and howling winds. Only very compact snow from a single fall could be used. It was cut into blocks that were light and easy to handle but would not crumble. A well-built *iglu* would last for one winter, as long as the temperature remained below freezing.

IGLU-VIGAS are still built today in the same way they always were. Firstly, a base of about three to five metres in diameter is marked out with a **snow knife** (see page 34). Blocks of snow are then built up in a spiral. The builder works from the inside, keeping the walls sloping inwards until a perfect dome is made. Then a small ventilation hole is cut out.

The entrance hole is cut and a domed entrance tunnel is built over it. The tunnel is made to slope downwards to keep out the icy winds. A few days later, when the structure has hardened, a window is cut and glazed with a pane of clear, freshwater ice.

A large platform of icy snow covered with furs serves as a bed. The family sleep in a row; the wife nearest to the lamp, her husband next to her and the children next to him.

FOR A KITCHEN TABLE they either used the floor, or built raised ice platforms. Cooking pots were hung over the oil lamp from a pole pushed into the walls. The lamp was filled with seal oil and was used for light, heat and cooking.

skis and ski poles

tunnel entrance stops icy winds from entering the living area

You will need: 2 polystyrene tiles (one with cotton wool glued all over the top for a base board), craft knife, scissors, PVA glue, thick card

1 Cut a flat ring from the card 2 cm wide. Cut a tapered strip from the plain tile, the same length as the circumference of the card ring.

2 Cut strip into blocks and glue to the card ring. They should slant inwards. Make the dome by cutting out more strips and blocks and gluing them on top of each other in a spiral pattern. Shape the last block to fit the top.

3 Cut a piece of tile to place inside *iglu* as a platform. Glue *iglu* to base.

4 Cut and glue blocks from the tile to make a domed entrance tunnel.

5 Cut a small arched doorway into the *iglu*. Glue tunnel over entrance. Glue wisps of cotton wool around the base and over the *iglu* to cover any cracks. Cut out a section as below if you want to see inside.

soft snow plastered to the outside of the iglu to seal gaps between the blocks

◁ *Hunters built iglus as temporary shelters while out on the sea ice.*

heat generated by people melts a thin layer of ice which then re-freezes, sealing the blocks on the inside

IN THE SUBARCTIC, people lived in tents all year round. These dwellings were generally kept warm in winter as people had access to wood and could make fires. In North America, Indians lived in tents of cleaned and smoked caribou or moose hide. The reindeer herders of the Siberian subarctic also used skin tents made of reindeer hide or fish skin, such as salmon.

THE PEOPLE OF SIBERIA lived in homes called yurts. In areas where the wood supply was plentiful, people built log yurts. But where animals such as sheep and goats were herded, a round wooden-framed tent with an outer covering of felt was used.

FELT IS MADE FROM WOOL that is not woven or knitted into a fabric, but is pounded until the matted fibres stick together. Thick felt is windproof, warm and waterproof and was also used to cover mattresses and cushions or to make wall hangings.

A FIRE BURNED in the centre of the yurt. A hole in the top of the dome allowed the smoke to escape. Around the fire, the yurt was divided into two parts. One half was occupied by the women with their kitchen utensils and knives for treating hides. In the other half, the men lived with their tools and weapons.

▷ *Yurts in southern Siberia were covered with warm layers of felt.*

EXTENDED FAMILIES often lived together in large yurts. Inside, there was a strict order which determined where people could sleep. The senior man of the group and his wife occupied the place of honour, which was furthest away from the door. Less important members of the family had to sleep closer to the door, where it was colder.

smoke hole

wood fire burns in centre of yurt

THE BASE OF THE YURT was made of wooden lattice-work, about a metre high. The frame was built in a circle and secured with pegs driven into the ground. The roof framework consisted of poles attached at one end to the lattice and at the other to a wooden ring that formed the smoke hole in the top of the dome.

crisscrossed frame gives greater stability

△ *People still live in yurts in some parts of Siberia. This picture shows a family gathered around a brazier, or stove, which has replaced the open fire.*

THE FELT COVERING for the yurt consisted of seven pieces. Four pieces were used to cover the lattice-work base, and two shaped sections covered the dome. The final section was a cover for the smoke hole, which could be removed if the yurt became too smoky or hot inside. The coverings were held in place with stones suspended by woollen bands.

woollen straps weighted with stones keep coverings in place in high winds

Moving with the seasons

Over the course of the year, most Eskimos experienced two major upheavals – the journey to and from the winter and summer settlements. In parts of the subarctic, this only involved short distances, whereas in the Arctic, some people crossed hundreds of kilometres to reach new hunting grounds.

THE SHORT AUTUMN arrives around September. During this time people hunted the last of the caribou and fished in the rivers before they froze over. Sled travel was impossible, as there was not enough snow on the ground, so journeys were done on foot, with dogs to carry equipment. Sea mammals were still hunted along the coast, but the ice was too thin to walk on. Camps were a hive of activity as people prepared for the coming winter: treating hides, drying meat, repairing sod houses and visiting neighbours.

permanent home of eastern Siberia

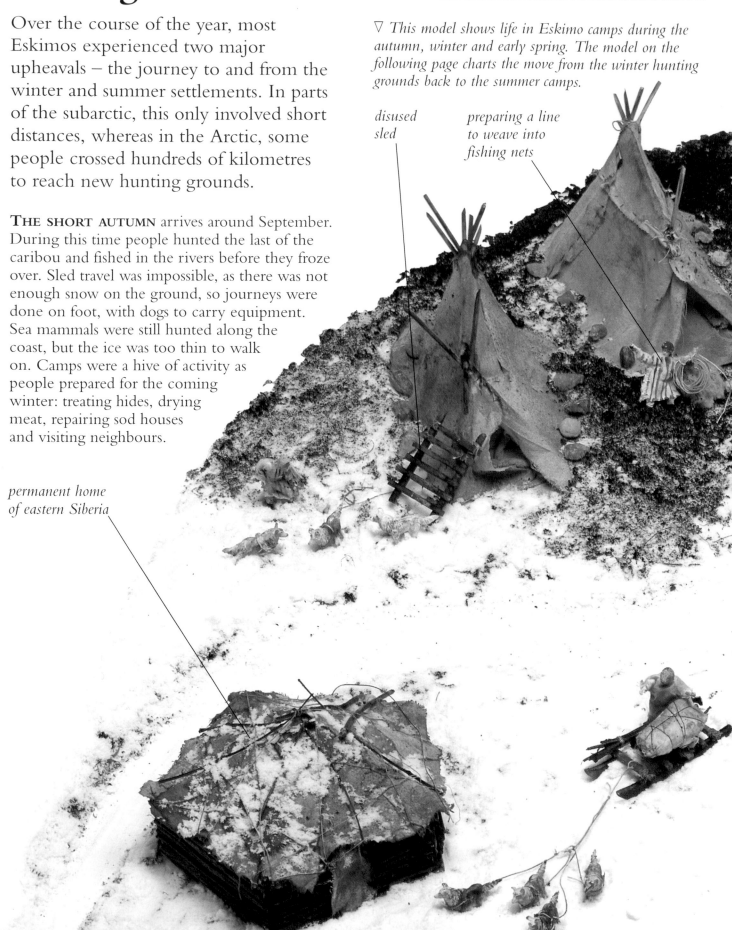

▽ *This model shows life in Eskimo camps during the autumn, winter and early spring. The model on the following page charts the move from the winter hunting grounds back to the summer camps.*

disused sled

preparing a line to weave into fishing nets

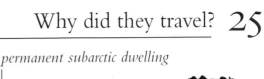

women stretch skins and dry meat

permanent subarctic dwelling

△ *Spring lasts from February to May. Once the sea ice begins to break up, it is time to trek back to the summer camps.*

temporary snowhouse on edge of ice floe

IN WINTER the land is whipped by gales and blizzards and cloaked in near darkness. Hunters travelled over the thick sea ice to catch seals and fish. They built *iglus* on the ice to stay close to the hunting grounds. When they were not hunting, families stayed in their sod houses or *iglus* telling stories, playing games, sewing clothes and carving.

LONGER DAYLIGHT HOURS mean that spring is arriving. For the Eskimos, spring was a time for making snares and collecting birds' eggs. As snow buntings (an arctic bird) and polar bears started to move about, they were hunted. As the ice became thinner, hunters made holes in the sea ice and caught cod and char, which were a welcome change from the winter diet of seal meat.

*men hunt whales along
the coast in boats called* **umiaks**

*kayak
in fast flowing
river – these boats
were used to hunt
migrating caribou*

BY LATE MAY OR JUNE, the ice had broken up. It was time to take to the open sea to hunt for whales, walrus and seal. As the rivers began to thaw, fish such as salmon returned from the sea in their thousands to spawn.

THE ESKIMOS who had lived in sod houses over the winter, moved back into skin tents for the summer. The tents kept out the wind and summer rains and offered some protection from the swarms of mosquitoes which infest the tundra in the summer. Smoky seal-oil lamps were usually placed at the entrance of the tent to keep the mosquitoes out.

IN THE EVENINGS, men repaired their kayaks and hunting gear, while the women mended clothing, and cleaned and prepared skins for clothes and sleeping bags.

SUMMER CAMPS were set up alongside rivers or on the coast. Younger men travelled great distances inland and hunted the migrating caribou which had returned to graze on the tundra.

caribou trapped in a corral by hunters

IN AUTUMN the weather becomes colder; lakes and rivers begin to freeze and the tundra is covered with thick frost. Caribou, birds, hares and foxes migrate south, signalling the arrival of winter. During August and September, the Eskimos trekked inland to hunt the last of the caribou. Then they carried the skins and meat back to the coast and waited for freeze-up.

IN OCTOBER it was time for the Eskimos to load up the sleds and return to the winter camps. They might rebuild the sod house they had abandoned the previous spring, or build a new one before the ground had frozen completely.

*meat buried in **caches** is left to mature*

Everyday life _____

There were no chiefs or rulers in Eskimo communities. People who needed advice consulted the elders, who were valued for their wisdom, their knowledge of customs and their ability to tell stories.

HOWEVER, WITHIN ARCTIC SETTLEMENTS there were two forms of leadership. A good hunter had the ability to keep a family well fed and was valued for his hunting skills. He would make the vital decision when to move to new hunting grounds. In times of hardship or hunger, people turned to the shaman, who was a holy man, for help. He would try to influence and control the evil spirits.

△ *A mother's parka was large enough to hold a baby in the back, which made carrying children over long distances easier.*

🐋 MAKE A TRAVEL BAG _____

 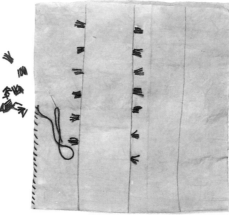 

You will need: calico, water paints, crayons, needle and thread, scraps of coloured wool, string, PVA glue

1 Cut out an oblong of calico about 90 cm x 45 cm. Make up a solution of 1 part glue to 10 parts water. Add some yellowy-brown paint.

2 Dip the calico into the solution so that it is completely covered. Wring and leave to dry.

3 Fold the material in half and sew up the side seams with coloured thread as above. Use a dark crayon to draw lines down the bag.

4 Glue snippets of coloured wool along the lines as shown above left.

5 Fold over the top edge of the bag and sew to make a hem. Leave a small gap to thread a drawstring through. Knot the ends of the drawstring to secure.

MEN HUNTED BIG GAME, constructed sod houses, *iglus* and boats, made tools, weapons and utensils and protected the family against physical danger. Hunting small game and birds was often shared between men and women.

WOMEN PROCESSED THE GAME AND HIDES, gathered vegetation, fished, prepared and cooked food, made clothes and ran the household. Both men and women had to learn the essential life-saving skill of sewing (see page 34).

△ *Aleut women decorated their sealskin bags, just as they did their clothes.*

△ *This picture shows a train of caribou sleds driven by the Nentsy people of Siberia. They still travel north for the spring migration, as they have done for many centuries.*

SHARING FOOD, SKILLS AND RESPONSIBILITIES was the basis for community life. In such small settlements, it was important that people were unselfish and treated each other with respect. Troublemakers were dealt with severely if they were persistent. At first, they were made fun of, to try to make them mend their ways. If joking didn't work then, as a last resort, they would be driven out of the camp.

MARRIAGE was a simple arrangement where a couple decided to live together. Sharing food was very important for survival in the Arctic. Husbands and wives often formed lifelong bonds with other couples so that they could share their supplies in lean times.

NAMING CHILDREN was an important ritual, as only infants with names were considered human (see page 55). If babies cried often, it was thought that they were unhappy with their name, so they were given a new one.

MOVING CAMP happened often, so possessions had to be light and easy to carry. Belongings were packed into travel bags and transported from camp to camp – whatever could not be carried was left behind. Adults and children alike could walk for days or weeks, if necessary, to a new camp.

Hunting at sea and on land

Hunting in the Arctic was dangerous and difficult and required enormous patience. Hunters wore charms to encourage the spirits of the animals to give themselves up and asked the spirits for the help of their ancestors. It was important to pay respect to the animals and thank them for allowing themselves to be caught. In this way their spirits could be released to return the following season in another body.

IN EARLY WINTER, hunters scratched holes in the ice and speared arctic fish, using a three-pronged spear called a **leister**. By midwinter, the ice thickened making fishing almost impossible.

SEA MAMMALS SCRATCH HOLES in the ice so that they can come to the surface for air. Hunters would wait by these breathing holes for seals to appear. These holes were often difficult to find, especially if they were covered with a layer of fresh snow. Hunters attracted the attention of the animals by scratching the surface of the ice with a special scratcher (see page 35). Women and children sometimes helped by scaring sea mammals away from unguarded holes to make sure that the animals surfaced where the hunter was waiting.

▽ *Aleut hunters from the western Arctic wore seal decoy helmets when hunting seals. The hunters would crawl across the ice on their stomachs and then pounce!*

WAITING FOR A SEAL TO SURFACE at a breathing hole could take days. As protection from the freezing winds on the ice floe, a hunter would build a windbreak out of snow and crouch behind it. He would have to concentrate all the time, so that he was ready to strike when the seal appeared.

MAKE A LEISTER

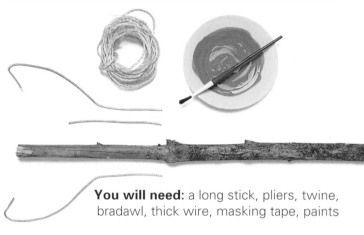

You will need: a long stick, pliers, twine, bradawl, thick wire, masking tape, paints

1 Ask an adult to help you cut the wire into 3 lengths, 2 x 20 cm and 1 x 15 cm. Use pliers to shape the longer, outer wires as shown.

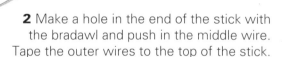

2 Make a hole in the end of the stick with the bradawl and push in the middle wire. Tape the outer wires to the top of the stick.

3 Wrap the twine around the end of the stick and in and out of the 3 prongs. For safety, cover the middle prong with masking tape. Paint the stick and twine to make them look like gut and bone.

IN SPRING, the *polynyas*, or areas of open sea which were hunted, expanded as the ice melted. Sea mammals were hunted from kayaks with harpoons. During the summer, sea mammals bask in the sun on the floating ice pans. Hunters would lie in wait on the ice pretending to be another basking seal and harpoon them when they got close.

WHEN THE SEA ICE BROKE UP, several hunters in kayaks, or eight hunters in one *umiak* would set out on the very dangerous business of whale and walrus hunting. The main supplies of sea mammal meat were collected from May to July, and later in early winter, when the sea had frozen once again and mammals were hunted on the ice.

BONE OR IVORY PEGS were used to plug an animal's wounds after it had been caught, so that the blood would not escape. Warm blood, which is rich in vitamins, was considered a great delicacy.

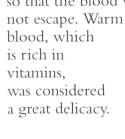

△ *In the spring, the rivers are full of spawning fish.*

IN THE WESTERN ARCTIC, nets were used to trap fish. They were either made from sealskin strips, shredded **baleen**, or shredded willow bark. Women made the thread then wove it into netting. The size of the mesh depended on the type of fish they were going to catch.

FISH such as salmon, arctic char and tom-cod were either caught on the ice with a line and hook, or by damming rivers as the fish swam upstream to spawn.

△ *On the ice, fish were lured with a line and bait, then speared with a leister: the centre prong pierced the fish, while the outer prongs held it in place.*

△ *Many Siberian peoples, such as the Eveny, Chukchi and Koryak, kept herds of caribou. The caribou provided their herders with milk, meat and hides, and could also be ridden.*

CARIBOU are wild North American reindeer. They spend the summer on the tundra and go south for the winter to the forests below the tree line. Hunters did not chase after caribou, as it was too exhausting for them to run in their heavy clothes. Instead, they would lay an ambush. In order to work out which route the caribou would take, the hunters studied the weather and used their knowledge of how the herds had behaved in the past. If that failed, they would consult a shaman.

▽ *These Copper Inuit men use distinctive curved bows and arrows made from wood and sinew. As caribou are curious and short-sighted animals, the hunters were able to get very close before shooting with deadly accuracy.*

WHEN SETTING AN AMBUSH, hunters knew that the caribou preferred to cross rivers and lakes at narrow, shallow points. They built corrals, or enclosures, in a huge V shape at the water's edge to drive the animals to one spot, where they were speared with lances by men in kayaks. To capture caribou on land, the animals were driven into a circular corral of poles where they would be trapped with snares, or fall into pits. Bows and arrows were used to pick off individual animals that were too widely spread out to be ambushed.

WATCHING FOR HERDS OF GAME required endless patience and warm clothing. The hunter sat motionless, scanning the horizon for the slightest movement. For the Eskimos, the landscape was alive; they believed that every rock and fold of land had a spirit that, if in a good mood, would help the hunter.

a hunter waits in the shallows to spear caribou

POLAR BEARS were highly prized arctic mammals. They were hunted in the late spring, when the mother bear was holed up in her den with her pups. Killing a polar bear required great skill and was cause for celebration. Their hides were very useful, but polar-bear meat, unless well cooked, was poisonous.

a caribou crosses at a narrow point in the river

a kayak moves swiftly through shallow waters

women and children scare the caribou

stone mounds, or cairns, built in the shape of humans help to divert the caribou

some caribou trapped in corrals

Hunting and household tools

Eskimos made weapons for hunting and tools for household chores. They did not make weapons designed for war – all their energy was directed into staying alive and keeping their communities well fed and healthy. The arctic hunter's clever use of different types of weapon allowed him access to every possible source of food the hostile environment had to offer.

🐋 **THE HARPOON** is an ingenious weapon that enabled the Eskimos to hunt fast, powerful sea mammals in deep seas. The key element was a detachable spear point, which was fixed to a long line with floats at one end. When the harpoon struck an animal, the point came free of the main shaft, leaving the animal attached to the line and floats. The floats acted as a drag, exhausting the wounded animal and preventing it from diving deeply. The hunter could then close in for the kill.

▷ *Bolas were thrown at flocks of flying birds to knock them out of the sky. The hunters wore their bolas wrapped around their heads, so they were always to hand when a flock of birds flew past.*

SNOW KNIVES were used for cutting blocks of wind-packed snow to make windbreaks, storage platforms and snowhouses. They were usually made of walrus ivory or bone.

🐋 MAKE A HARPOON

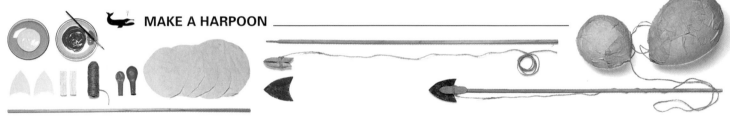

You will need: 2 balsa wood blocks 6 cm long x 2 cm wide x 1.5 cm deep, 1 dowel 1 cm thick x 1 m long, craft knife, balloons, calico, PVA glue, string, cardboard, sandpaper, paint

1 Ask an adult to help you shape the wood pieces as shown. Sandpaper and paint. Cut card into 2 spearhead shapes, glue together and paint grey.

2 Ask an adult to whittle one end of the dowel to the shape as shown above, so the two balsa wood pieces fit neatly on to either side of it.

3 Use the string to loosely bind the balsa wood blocks together. Glue the card spearhead in between the blocks and tighten the string. Fit the spearhead assembly on to the dowel.

4 Now make the bladder floats. Blow up 2 balloons and cover with patches of calico stuck with glue.

5 Paint the calico a brown colour to look like sealskin. Leave to dry. Wind the string, which is attached to the spearhead, around the dowel. Then tie the bladder floats to the string.

◁ *Sewing tools and fasteners for needlework bags were highly decorative, reflecting the importance of the needle.*

THE NEEDLE was the most important household tool of all, as both men and women needed to know how to sew waterproof seams. These fragile items were made of bird bone or walrus ivory and stored in highly decorated cases for safekeeping.

BOWS were made of wood or, in the eastern Arctic, antlers, and bound with sinew. Arrows had wooden shafts and long bone points. Bows and arrows were used for both hunting and fishing.

harpoon with line and seal-bladder float

▽ *The harpoon was used by hunters to attach a line to their sea-mammal prey. Harpoons had detachable 'toggle' heads which twisted sideways under the animal's skin, and could not be pulled out, even by a whale or a walrus.*

△ *As seals are attracted to strange sounds, arctic hunters made ice-scratchers to scrape on the ice to lure seals to within harpoon range.*

KNIVES AND ADZES, with sharpened and shaped stone or metal blades and bone handles, were used for carving and cutting up carcasses. Picks were made of walrus tusks and wood, and were used for digging up edible roots in summer.

LANCES, or spears, have blades that are permanently attached to their shafts. They were designed to kill animals at close quarters. Sharp-bladed lances often have sheaths to protect the blade and prevent accidents.

NET-MAKING TOOLS were used by women to weave fishing nets of different sizes. It was a very time-consuming process – almost a whole year was needed to make the line and weave it into netting. The materials, either shredded willow bark, shredded baleen, or sealskin strips, were collected in summer and weaving started in the winter. Finally, all the individual nets would be sewn together to make one large net.

Getting around

Eskimos had to journey across land, sea and rivers in their search for food. They built different types of transport to help them, each suited to a particular purpose. The kayak was both a travelling and hunting craft. Light and easy to manoeuvre, it enabled the hunter to approach his prey and to pursue it stealthily through the water. It had a very shallow draft or depth, so it could be used in the shallow points of the river where caribou liked to cross. It was also light enough to be picked up and carried when reaching land.

△ *This Inuit in northwest Greenland is hunting in a closed-deck kayak for seal or walrus. Two seal-bladder floats are positioned behind him.*

MAKE A KAYAK

You will need: wooden fruit box, thin card, tissue paper, paint, varnish, cardboard tube, craft knife, PVA glue

1 Ask an adult to help cut a 10 mm wide x 30 cm long keel (the angled piece forming the base of the boat).

2 Cut 5 thin strips slightly longer than the keel, and a paddle from the box. Trim the ends of 2 thin strips (stringers) at an angle to join the keel. Glue in place. Cut, trim and glue the other ends, bending stringers slightly outwards as above.

3 Now fix the 2 lower stringers in the same way. The outward bow on these should be narrower than that of the upper stringers. Cut 4 mm-wide ribs from thin card and glue into position as shown. End ribs are V-shaped; central ones, U-shaped.

arctic kayak with sealskin covering

 SUBARCTIC INDIAN CANOES had a similar design to arctic kayaks, except they had open tops. Instead of sealskin, the Indians sewed birch bark on to wooden frames and waterproofed the boats with gummy tree sap.

KAYAK FRAMES were made of driftwood or whalebone, held together with sinew and baleen. The frame was made exactly to fit the owner, and was usually six metres long and one metre wide.

SEALSKINS with the fur removed, were used for making kayaks. They were soaked, stretched and sewn together with sinew. Seal oil was applied to make the craft waterproof.

◁ *The ulu is a knife with a curved slate or metal blade and an ivory or bone handle. It was used by women to clean hides for making everything from clothes to kayaks.*

A KAYAK IS PROPELLED with a single or double-paddled blade. The double-paddled blade gives extra speed. In Alaska, paddle blades were sometimes decorated with symbols that identified the owners and gave them magic powers.

TO PROTECT THEIR KAYAKS from the sled dogs (who, if given the chance, would chew them to pieces), the Eskimos built high, stone platforms. The kayaks were stored on these until needed.

IN REGIONS WHERE wood was too scarce to make the larger cargo boats, or *umiaks*, two or more kayaks were lashed together and used as a raft for carrying goods and people. In Alaska, two kayaks were sometimes tied together and fitted with a mast and sail. They were very stable in heavy seas, unlike the single kayak, which is not suited to rough seas. When travelling inland for the caribou hunting season, the hunter would carry his kayak upside down on his shoulders.

ALEUT KAYAKS were often decorated with sea otter charms carved from ivory or bone. They were sewn on to the sides of the boat to appease the spirits of dead sea mammals and encourage others to give themselves to the hunters.

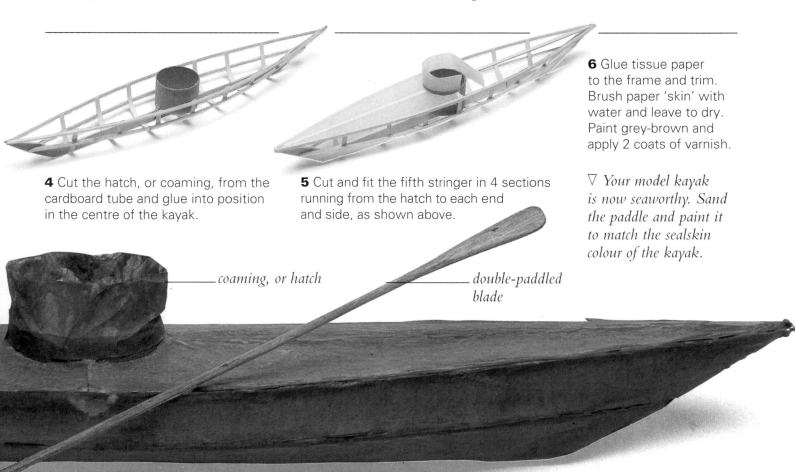

6 Glue tissue paper to the frame and trim. Brush paper 'skin' with water and leave to dry. Paint grey-brown and apply 2 coats of varnish.

4 Cut the hatch, or coaming, from the cardboard tube and glue into position in the centre of the kayak.

5 Cut and fit the fifth stringer in 4 sections running from the hatch to each end and side, as shown above.

▽ *Your model kayak is now seaworthy. Sand the paddle and paint it to match the sealskin colour of the kayak.*

—— *coaming, or hatch*

—— *double-paddled blade*

WATERPROOF COWLINGS, or 'vests' made of sealskin were often fixed to the hatch of arctic kayaks. The cowling was pulled up and over the occupant to prevent water from splashing in.

SITTING IN A KAYAK all day with legs stretched out could be very tiring. Boys did exercises to stretch the muscles in their legs to help them get used to this uncomfortable position.

THE UMIAK was used both for carrying belongings and for whale hunting. Like the kayak it had a frame of wood or whalebone and a covering of sealskin or walrus hide. It was about nine metres long, could carry a load of 900 kilos plus eight passengers and yet, unloaded, it could be picked up and carried by four men. These boats were very stable and therefore could be rowed or sailed in very rough seas.

△ These people are getting ready to launch an umiak. Sometimes boxes full of charms were carried in the boat to ensure the hunters were successful and came to no harm.

MOST WHALE HUNTING took place during the brief summer when the ice floe had broken up. Umiaks were re-covered or patched in March. As the time approached when the whales returned to their feeding grounds, the boats were moved to the ice edge, ready to be launched when whales were spotted.

SKILLED HUNTERS in a 10-metre umiak could hunt a bowhead whale which was twice as long. It took great courage, as a whale could easily upturn an umiak, but it was worth the risk. One whale could supply as much **blubber** as 1,000 seals and, when wood was scarce, whalebones served as tent poles and sled runners. Whales were not killed outright. They were harpooned, usually several times, and prevented from diving too deeply by the seal floats attached to the harpoon heads. Then the hunters would close in and kill the whale with their lances.

A WHALE HUNTING PARTY would consist of several umiaks. When a whale was sighted, they would circle the beast, waiting for it to resurface so that they could harpoon and lance it.

AN UMIALIK was the owner and head of a whaling boat. All whalers were respected, but an umialik was especially highly regarded, because he was seen as a great provider for his family and the village.

▷ This umiak is ready to sail in search of whales.

boom

shrouds, or stays

bow, or front   harpoon

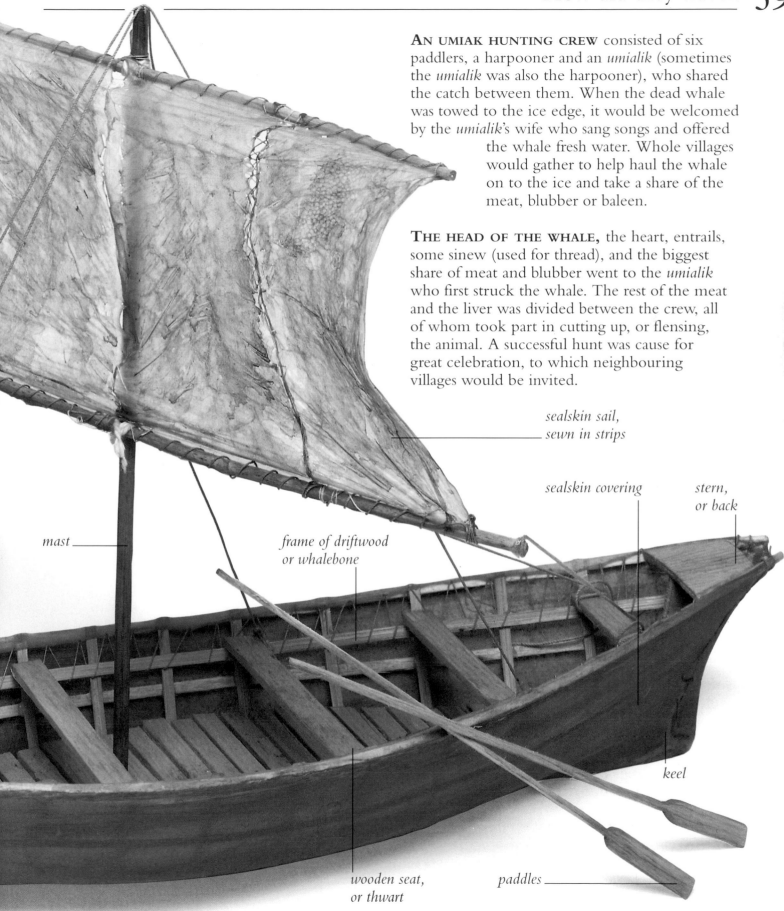

AN UMIAK HUNTING CREW consisted of six paddlers, a harpooner and an *umialik* (sometimes the *umialik* was also the harpooner), who shared the catch between them. When the dead whale was towed to the ice edge, it would be welcomed by the *umialik*'s wife who sang songs and offered the whale fresh water. Whole villages would gather to help haul the whale on to the ice and take a share of the meat, blubber or baleen.

THE HEAD OF THE WHALE, the heart, entrails, some sinew (used for thread), and the biggest share of meat and blubber went to the *umialik* who first struck the whale. The rest of the meat and the liver was divided between the crew, all of whom took part in cutting up, or flensing, the animal. A successful hunt was cause for great celebration, to which neighbouring villages would be invited.

sealskin sail, sewn in strips

sealskin covering

stern, or back

mast

frame of driftwood or whalebone

keel

wooden seat, or thwart

paddles

MOVING ACROSS LAND was an exhausting business, especially in summer when sleds could not be used due to the lack of snow. Instead, people trekked on foot, carrying their possessions. They only took what was needed, such as bows and arrows, seal-oil lamps and tents. The elders of the community often remained in the coastal settlements. In spring, bone or ivory **crampons** were lashed to boot soles to make walking on the ice easier.

▷ *Dog teams were either hitched to the sled in a fan formation as pictured, or in a long single line.*

THE TOBOGGAN was invented by the Cree Indians of North America. It consisted of a flat piece of wood or frozen skin that was laden with goods and pulled over the ice. A similar version was also used in Siberia.

▷ *This sled is from the eastern Arctic.*

grab rail

THE SLED is a raised platform on two runners, developed by the Eskimo. It was faster than the toboggan and could take heavier loads. The runners were often lined with strips of walrus ivory or baleen, then rubbed with a soil-and-water paste which froze solid. To add a glaze, the Eskimos spat water on to the runners, which froze inmediately.

MAKE A SLED

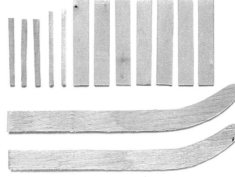

You will need: wooden fruit box, PVA glue, craft knife, fur scraps

1 Ask an adult to help you cut out 2 runners, 12 cm long x 10 mm deep, from the fruit box. Then cut enough strips of planking 5 cm long x 1 cm wide to cover the sled.

2 Cut out 5 strips, 3 mm x 4 cm, as shown above left. The grab rails are 4 cm long; the supports, 4.5 cm long.

3 Glue the short planks in position across the runners, until the whole base is covered. Make sure there are no gaps between the planks.

4 Now assemble the grab rail, angling the longer strips so that they support the uprights as shown.

5 Load up your sled with fur bundles. If you rub the bottoms of the runners with candle wax, it should glide through snow.

SLEDS WERE USED to transport belongings to and from the winter and summer hunting grounds, and to carry the spoils from the hunt. They were made from either driftwood, or bone and antler, depending on what was available. If these were in short supply, fish wrapped in sealskin were frozen in the shape of runners.

HUSKY DOGS are native to all areas of the Arctic and were heavily relied upon by the Eskimos. Huskies were trained to find breathing holes in the ice, corral caribou, haul carcasses back to camp and pull sleds. Six dogs could pull a lightweight wooden sled, but up to 16 might be needed for a heavier bone-and-skin model.

THE SAAMIS invented skis for getting around on snow. They were basically pieces of driftwood or bone, treated with soil and water like the underside of sled runners, and lashed to their boots.

MAKE A PAIR OF SKIS AND SKI STICKS

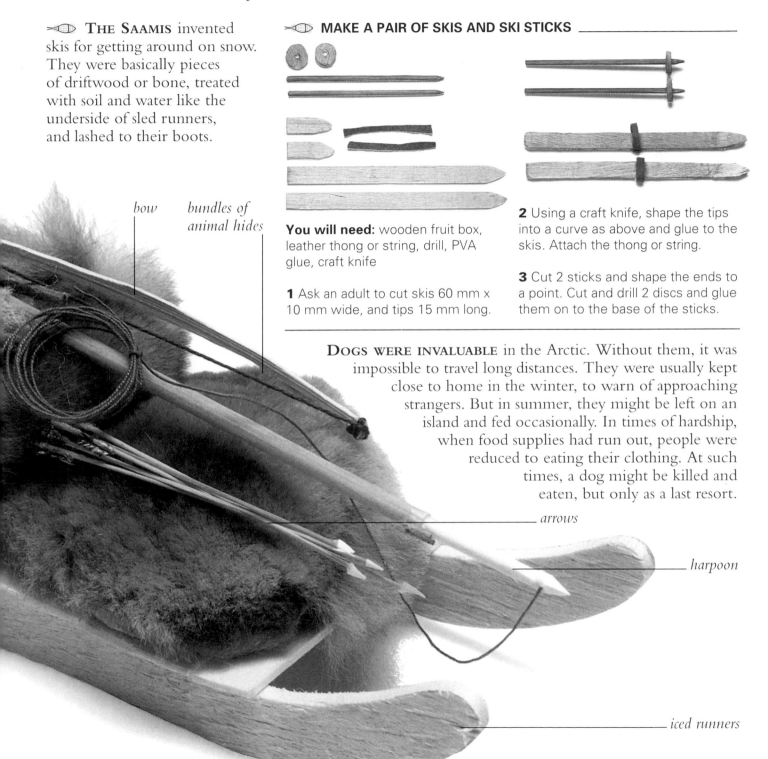

bow

bundles of animal hides

You will need: wooden fruit box, leather thong or string, drill, PVA glue, craft knife

1 Ask an adult to cut skis 60 mm x 10 mm wide, and tips 15 mm long.

2 Using a craft knife, shape the tips into a curve as above and glue to the skis. Attach the thong or string.

3 Cut 2 sticks and shape the ends to a point. Cut and drill 2 discs and glue them on to the base of the sticks.

DOGS WERE INVALUABLE in the Arctic. Without them, it was impossible to travel long distances. They were usually kept close to home in the winter, to warn of approaching strangers. But in summer, they might be left on an island and fed occasionally. In times of hardship, when food supplies had run out, people were reduced to eating their clothing. At such times, a dog might be killed and eaten, but only as a last resort.

arrows

harpoon

iced runners

The arctic diet

There were very few vegetables or fruits, no grains to make bread and no starchy food such as potatoes. The Eskimo diet consisted almost entirely of meat and fish. They kept healthy by eating every part of the animal. They ate the fat, eyes, organs, stomach contents and blood to give them all the minerals, vitamins and fibre they needed on this high-protein diet. For variety, they matured pieces of meat for a stronger flavour – just as we eat strong blue cheese. Matured seal-flipper was much prized as a tasty morsel.

▷ *This Nentsy girl is cooking over an open fire. When wood was available, food was often grilled and roasted.*

BANNOCK is a type of bread which was introduced to the Eskimos by Scottish whalers. The original recipe used water, but in the recipe below we have used yoghurt for more flavour.

MAKE BANNOCK BREAD

You will need: 450 g plain flour, 1 tsp salt, 1 tsp bicarbonate of soda, 300 ml plain yoghurt or buttermilk, a large frying pan with a lid, oil for cooking

1 Sift together the flour, salt and bicarbonate of soda in a large bowl.

2 Add the yoghurt or buttermilk to the flour mixture and mix into a soft dough, adding water if necessary.

3 Turn out the dough on to a floured board and knead for 5 minutes. Form into rolls. Ask an adult to oil the pan and place it over a medium heat.

4 Add rolls to the pan, cover and reduce the heat. After 3 minutes, turn the rolls over, replace the lid and cook for another 3 minutes until the rolls are golden brown. Leave to cool.

FRESH WATER was obtained from melted ice, or from snow. Eskimos preferred to melt ice, because snow, which is made up almost entirely of air, takes a long time to melt and large quantities are needed just to make a little water.

FOOD WAS COOKED in a cauldron suspended over a seal-oil lamp or, in regions where wood was available, over an open fire. A hunk of meat or fish was usually boiled in water, and the remaining liquid made a nutritious soup.

IN SUMMER, in parts of the southern Arctic, berries, edible leaves and roots added variety to the Eskimo's basic diet of meat and fish. Seaweed was also eaten in parts of southern Alaska.

FOOD WAS PRESERVED by drying it in the sun and air, or by freezing. Drying could only be done during the warm summer months. Meat was cut into strips and left outside for a couple of days, then packed into bags of seal blubber. Meat or fish prepared in this way lasted almost a year. Frozen meat did not last as long as dried, and a lamp was needed to defrost it. If lamps were not available, frozen meat was chewed. Food was often stored in the ice until required.

▽ *Bannock became a staple food for the Eskimos, making them dependent on supplies of flour brought in by European and American traders.*

SEA MAMMAL FAT was used for all sorts of things. Chunks of it made an enjoyable snack. If it was left and kept away from sunlight it turned into clear liquid. This was used to light and heat Eskimo homes, and was used as a medicine, a skin cream and insect repellent in the summer.

FISH AND SHELLFISH were a vital source of food, as were waterfowl and birds which nested on the cliff edges. The most important types of fish, such as salmon and char, are migratory, and therefore only available for a short season.

MEAL TIMES were not fixed; people ate when they were hungry. Food was laid out on the floor and the hunter made the first cut. After that, everyone helped themselves, using their own knives to cut off portions of meat.

Fun and games

Children were encouraged to play with toys that would give them the skills they needed later on in life. Girls were given dolls to dress so they could practise sewing. Boys were given slingshots and toy bows and arrows, so they could learn how to hunt. Strenuous games kept adult hunters fit when the weather was too bad to go outside. Other games, such as *ayagag*, were perfect for playing indoors during the long winter.

AUTUMN WAS THE FESTIVE SEASON. It was a time for gathering together before the ice was firm enough to hunt on. Families sent out messengers asking other allied families to join them for feasts. These were called messenger feasts. The invited family would set out laden with food and gifts for their hosts. The round trip could take up to six weeks.

△ *Nentsy boys learn to hunt at an early age. This boy is using a small bow and arrow made specially for him.*

KICKBALL was a kind of football. It was played by two teams who tried to win possession of the ball and score a goal. The pitch could be any size and the goal areas were simply marked in the ground. Any number of people could play, adults and children alike.

MAKE A KICKBALL

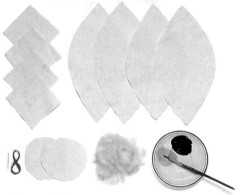  

18

You will need: calico, scissors, paint, needle and thread, kapok or other filling material, paint

1 Cut 4 calico squares 9 cm x 9 cm, and 2 circles, 9 cm in diameter.

2 Cut 4 oval sections of calico as shown above left, 20 cm long x 14 cm across at the widest point.

3 Paint the squares and circles brown with white patterns as shown.

4 Sew the oval sections together, leaving one side open. Pack the ball with stuffing and sew up the last seam. Paint a yellow-brown colour and leave to dry. Stitch on the patterned squares and circles.

IN TOUCHBALL, a player had to jump and kick a sealskin ball suspended from the ceiling, using one or both feet. Male athletes could kick as high as three metres, women over two metres.

THE FINGER PULL was rather like arm wrestling. Opponents faced one another, with their right toes touching. They hooked the middle fingers of their right hands and tried to pull each other off balance.

MAKE AN AYAGAG

You will need: string, self-hardening clay, thin dowel, craft knife, paint

1 Ask an adult to help you sharpen the end of a piece of dowel. Make a flat disc of clay and poke holes in it with the end of the dowel, making some holes larger than others.

2 Paint the clay disc brown to look like bone. Leave to dry and then tie one end of the string to the disc and the other end to the dowel as shown.

To play the game, use the stick to toss the disc into the air, and try to catch the disc on the stick. You will score more points for spearing the disc through the smaller holes.

BLANKET TOSS was a favourite sport among young people. A blanket made of walrus skins was held at the edges by many people and pulled tight like a trampoline. One person got on the blanket and was thrown high up into the air – up to 10 metres. The most acrobatic performers could do twists, turns and somersaults, and points were awarded according to their skill.

△ *This blanket-toss game was held in Nome, Alaska, in 1955.*

TO MAKE A KICKBALL (known as an *unkak* in Alaska), soft sealskin was stitched and stuffed with caribou hair or moss. The ball varied in size, but was usually no bigger than 12–15 cm. It was also decorated with symbols.

◁ *Kickball was played by children and young men at the end of winter, or in spring.*

DANCING took place in the *kashims*, or men's houses. These were large, communal homes where men sometimes spent the day dancing, singing and drumming. In the western Arctic, dances were elaborate and had set movements. In the eastern Arctic, events such as bear hunts were acted out and these dances varied more according to the dancer's mood than those in the west. Men's dances were jumpy and jerky. Women danced less strenuously, swaying from the waist and moving their upper bodies and arms.

△ *Contests of strength were very popular at festivals.*

MAKE A STORY KNIFE

You will need: cardboard, scissors, strips of newspaper, wallpaper paste, sandpaper, paint

1 Cut a knife shape from cardboard and cover with layers of newspaper and wallpaper paste. Leave to dry.

2 Smooth the surface with fine-grade sandpaper. Paint an ivory colour and decorate with black or brown paint.

△ *Cat's cradle was a popular game, played with string, that accompanied stories and songs. Eskimos knew how to make hundreds of shapes, each with its own name.*

STORY KNIVES made of wood, bone or walrus ivory, were used to draw pictures and symbols in the snow or mud, to illustrate storytellers' tales.

STORIES WERE TOLD IN SONG – men sang the stories and women sang the chorus. The most popular stories were about the spirit world and how animals were created, or shamans' tales of the past. Some songs were treated as the private property of a person, while others belonged to a whole family, or to the community. Often people had their own individual songs with lyrics that described their feelings, or events in their lives.

SINGING was an important form of expression for arctic peoples. Eskimos sang while they worked, danced and played with their children. People used song to settle arguments and sometimes had singing contests between the feuding parties in which the audience judged who was right or wrong. Songs were also used to work magic by enlisting the help of the spirit world. Some of the Eskimo songs were of ancient origin, while others were specially composed for certain events or made up on the spot.

◁ *A **bow-drill** was used to carve designs on the story knife. Birds and fish were popular motifs.*

bow-drill

ivory carvings

Stories and symbols

The Eskimos had no written language, so family histories were kept alive through storytelling. The arctic peoples, although scattered into thousands of tiny settlements, spoke three basic languages: Aleut, Yupik and Inuit. The arctic language is rich in the way it expressed feelings and ideas and how it described the natural world. For instance, the Inuit language has approximately 70 words to describe different types of snow.

FAMILY HISTORY was told and retold through generations. However, it is thought that some carvings were made to record past events in picture form.

△ *The missionaries brought their own languages, such as Russian and English, to the arctic region and many foreign words are present in the Inuit language today.*

MISSIONARIES, eager to convert the native peoples to Christianity, followed in the wake of the fur traders, whalers and explorers. Between them, these groups disrupted and destroyed the traditional way of life in the Arctic. But the missionaries did do some good. They helped to preserve the main languages and many of the **dialects** by working out a way to record them.

△ *This Eveny woman is using a traditional wooden calendar. It was introduced by the Russian Orthodox church to help people remember important feast days.*

🏠 🐋 **UNTIL THE EUROPEANS ARRIVED,** most Inuits could not count beyond five or six, because they did not need to. Any amount over this was simply called 'many'. Their year was divided into several seasons, rather than weeks or days. The words for the seasons were very descriptive: February was *Koblut*, which means 'ground cracked by frost'; June was known as *Munilut* or egg month, while *Qononilut* was September, or the fading month.

🏠 **THE INUIT LANGUAGE** consists of core words that build up to become other words by adding endings, or suffixes. This example uses the core word *qiqi* (frozen):

qiqijuk	=	frozen
qiqitirpuq	=	he has frozen his feet or, part of his foot is frozen
qiqiqralijarnatuq	=	snow which is squeaky or crunchy underfoot

🐟 **THE SUBARCTIC INDIANS** have many words to explain the weather. For example, the Cree refer to the four winds as brothers and give each one a character. This is how three of them are described:

West wind (*Nikapi-hun-nizeo*) – A favourable person, good and generous to mankind. The best hunting wind.
East wind (*Wapanung-nizeo*) – A stingy fellow, he starves the people, and will give them nothing to eat.
South wind (*Shawanung-nizeo*) – Gives food in summer, and has charge of it. He gives the berries.

▷ *Written Inuit is based on syllables, or units, which combine to make a word.*

△ *This is the Inuit language in written form. It was devised by James Evans, a missionary.*

🏠 **TO WRITE IN INUIT,** look at the chart above. Words can be made up by combining syllables and 'finals', which are shown in the far right column. These represent the sound made by the first letter of the syllables shown in the first three columns. For example:

Δᶜᗐ = *iglu* (home)

Arts and crafts of the Arctic

For most of the year, Eskimos had little time to devote to purely decorative crafts. However, during the two to three months of continuous darkness in winter, men and women spent many hours perfecting their skills in making clothes, weapons and artefacts. Practically every man and woman was in some sense an artist, and well-crafted objects were much admired. Eskimos saw no difference between making things that were useful, beautiful, or religious. Instead, all these qualities were combined when making even the most ordinary of things, from a hairpin to a fish hook or clothes basket.

△ *These Aleut baskets, on sale at a trading post, were made by hand. They were woven from dune grass, gathered on the coast during the summer months.*

JEWELLERY, such as earrings, necklaces and belts, was often made with a base of softened sealskin. Animal teeth and walrus ivory were used to decorate the skin, along with feathers, birds' claws and bills. Ivory or bone beads were also used and, later, glass **tradebeads** became popular.

SUBARCTIC SIBERIANS, such as the Koryak, made bracelets, earrings and pendants from iron, brass and copper. The Eveny people wore brass pendants called 'throat medals' tied around their necks with leather thongs. The pendants were believed to protect the wearer from colds.

MAKE A BASKET

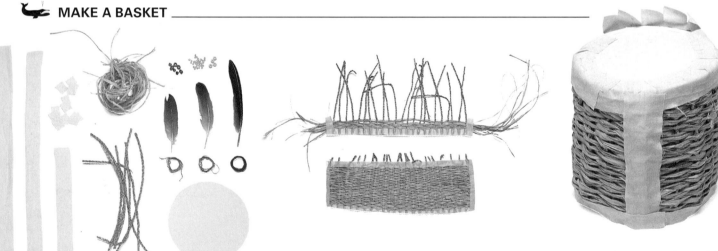

You will need: twine cut into 25 cm lengths, raffia, masking tape, needle and different coloured thread, card, calico strips 3 cm wide x 40 cm long, small calico squares, paint, glue, beads, feathers, scissors

1 Cut a piece of masking tape about 40 cm long. Stick down lengths of twine about 1.5 cm apart. Tape this row of twine to your work surface.

2 Now weave raffia in and out of the twine until you have a woven piece measuring about 25 cm x 40 cm.

3 Tape the edges of the weaving with masking tape. Then bend the weaving around to form a tube. Place the tube on card, draw a circle to fit the base. Cut this out and tape over the base.

4 Glue calico strips around the joins at the base, the rim and the seam.

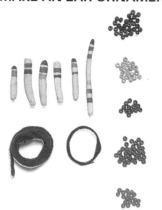

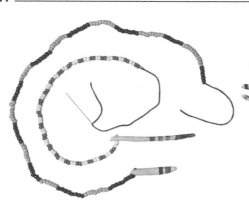

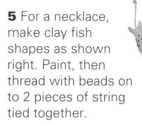

You will need: small glass beads, coloured thread, paint, thick wool, self-hardening clay, needle

1 Make 8 long thin beads out of the clay. Make a hole in the top of each one and leave to dry. Paint as above.

2 Thread 4 strands of beads, making patterns with the colours as above. Tie the long beads on to the ends.

3 Tie up the strands with two lengths of wool. Tie the wool lengths to form a loop and hook over each ear.

5 For a necklace, make clay fish shapes as shown right. Paint, then thread with beads on to 2 pieces of string tied together.

ALEUT BASKET MAKERS also used one of the most unusual of all basket-weaving materials – fibres from the baleen of the bowhead whale, a type of whale that lives by filtering plankton out of seawater. Baleen baskets had ivory lid handles carved in the shape of a seal or whale's tail. They were popular items for trade.

THE PACIFIC ALEUTS of southwest Alaska, made baskets that were mainly used for carrying fish. The grasses were split with the fingernails into strands as thin as silk threads. Some strands were dyed to weave patterns into the baskets.

▷ *Baskets like these were used for storing precious household possessions and clothes.*

5 Paint the small calico squares with bright colours as shown. Then glue them on to the basket. Thread the string with several coloured beads and sew these on. Decorate the seams with patterns made from coloured threads, and stitch some feathers around the top.

CARVED FIGURES were made for both religious and decorative purposes. Eskimos believed that every figure, human or animal, was possessed with a spirit. Even ordinary household objects were decorated with likenesses of these spirits. Ivory buttons were carved with human faces, needlecases in the shape of women, belt buckles like seals, and bowls in the form of birds or sea mammals.

SCULPTURES AND MASKS were carved from wood, if available, and from walrus ivory, bone and antler horn using carving knives and a bow-drill. Patterns were also cut or drilled out of stone.

KNIVES AND BURINS, a type of engraving tool, were used to carve tiny pictures on the smallest and most awkward objects, such as beads and arrow shafts. The bow-drill had a fine bit made of flint, copper or iron, and it meant that narrow holes could be drilled precisely in tough materials.

△ *Mask-like faces were carved on earrings and bladder-float plugs. These ones have human and animal features: the smiling face is male, the frowning face is female.*

MODERN ESKIMO ARTISTS have adopted a new technique. Since 1958, they have been carving out of stone to produce prints, such as the one shown below. In one method, the design is carved out of a flat stone, ink is applied to the surface and then paper or sealskin is placed over the stone and rubbed so that the design is transferred. Modern printmakers use many traditional patterns, such as birds and animals, as a basis for their designs.

MAKE AN ESKIMO PRINT

You will need: paper, tracing paper, pencil, several polystyrene tiles, craft knife, paint, sponge, fabric

1 Draw a design, made up of four or five sections, on to paper.

2 Trace each section of the design on to a separate polystyrene block. Ask an adult to help you cut away the polystyrene around the outline of each part of the design as above. (We have outlined the raised part of the design in black so you can see it.)

3 Repeat the process described in step 2 until all sections of your design have been cut out. Then dab your chosen colours on to the separate printing blocks with a piece of sponge. Apply the paint evenly, covering the whole design.

◁ *Spoons and bowls were often beautifully decorated with creatures from Eskimo myths and legends. These are Yupik skeleton-style pictures: caribou on the bowl and a seal on the spoon.*

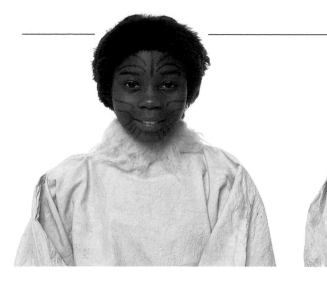

TATTOOING was a common form of decoration for Eskimo women. It was also a sign that girls were ready to marry. The tattoos were made by threading a sooty string just under the surface of the skin, a process which could be uncomfortable. The chin, nose, cheeks, legs and arms were the most popular parts of the body for tattooing.

WOODEN BOXES were carved with the animals and objects on which the Eskimos depended for their survival. It was a way of honouring their spirits. Sometimes a carving of a small animal, perhaps a baby seal, served as a lid or handle. Boxes were often inlaid with ivory or coloured beads.

TOBACCO became an important item in trade and the Eskimos made many beautiful objects associated with it. Pipes and snuff boxes were elaborately carved from materials such as antler, wood and ivory.

4 Print your picture by pressing each block firmly on to some fabric or paper as above. You might want to practise on scrap paper first. Leave to dry, then the finished picture is ready to frame.

▷ *The finished polystyrene print shown here is called The Enchanted Owl. It is copied from an artist called Kenojuak who comes from Cape Dorset on Baffin Island in the eastern Arctic.*

The spirit world

Eskimos believed that human spirits, names and characters were endlessly recycled. When death occurred, the spirit of the deceased entered a vast spirit world. It remained there until it was reborn in another human who took the spirit's name.

THINGS THAT WERE NOT LIVING were thought to have a spirit which gave them energy to do things. They also had a character which made them behave in certain ways. For instance, rocks might fall on, and even kill, animals or people who offended them by approaching in a disrespectful way.

MAKE A MASK

You will need: balloon, newspaper, wallpaper paste, thin card, scissors, sandpaper, paint and brushes, twigs, string, feathers, glue, tape

1 Blow up the balloon. Cover one half with several layers of newspaper strips soaked in wallpaper paste. Leave to dry. Pop the balloon and trim mask edges. Cut away a small section at the bottom of the mask.

2 Cut a semicircle from the card. Tape this to the bottom of mask to form the chin as shown above left. Cut out the eye holes with a pair of scissors. Cover the whole mask and chin with more layers of newspaper and paste. Leave to dry thoroughly.

MASKS were important in arctic culture. Some looked like humans or animals; some were comic caricatures; others represented ideas or spirits. The designs of masks were based on visions which the shamans had. When the mask was worn, the wearer temporarily took on the spirit of the character of the mask. They were used for feasts, dances and religious ceremonies.

◁ *Women danced with finger masks on their hands. Finger masks were trimmed with feathers or fur which waved about as they moved their hands.*

The Chukchi peoples of Siberia have this saying:
'All that exists lives. The lamps walk around. The walls of the houses have voices of their own... The skins sleeping in the bags talk at night. The antlers lying on the tomb arise at night and walk in procession around the mounds while the dead get up and visit the living.'

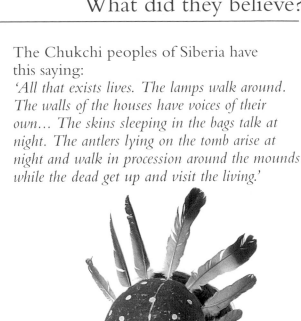

3 Smooth the surface with sandpaper. Paint and decorate the mask with twigs and feathers. To wear, make 2 small holes either side of the mask, about halfway up. Thread string through the holes and tie around the back of your head.

LIVING BEINGS had a soul, a shape and a character. They also had breath. This was something that gave people and animals a special ability to relate to the **Spirit of the Air**, the most powerful force in the world. It was this power that put people above plants and rocks.

A NAME was special and had its own power. Only humans had a name, so this put them above animals. When a person died, their name was given to the next infant to be born into the group – whether it was a boy or girl. Names were so special that once given, they were rarely used. People adopted nicknames instead.

ANIMALS' SPIRITS had to be calmed when the animal was killed, and some token offered in gratitude for giving up one of its lives. Either its likeness would be carved on to something, or part of it might be thrown back into the sea.

THE SHAMAN was a man or woman in touch with the spirits. Although every Eskimo knew how to deal with the spirit world, the shaman was especially powerful. His soul could leave his body and roam around the spirit world, seeking answers or advice from other spirits.

The shaman's role in the community was to tell tales of the spirits, to talk to the spirits in prayer, to cast spells and to heal the sick. A good shaman could even see into the future. The shaman performed most of his or her tasks in song and dance, and used a drum in accompaniment.

MAKE A SHAMAN'S DRUM

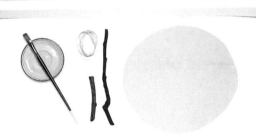

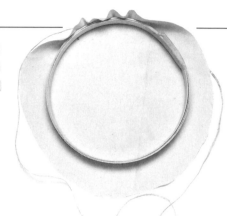

You will need: thick card, glue, strong tape, calico, scissors, craft knife, short stick, string, PVA glue, poster paints

1 Cut 3 strips of thick card 1 m long and 5 cm wide as above.

2 Glue strips on top of one another. Then bend into a circle and secure with strong tape.

3 Place the card circle on to calico. Cut out a larger circle of calico, so that it drapes over the card frame.

4 Ask an adult to help you make a hole in the card circle with the craft knife. Glue in the thick twig.

5 Pull calico tight over card frame. Tie around with string. Mix paint with PVA glue and paint the drum.

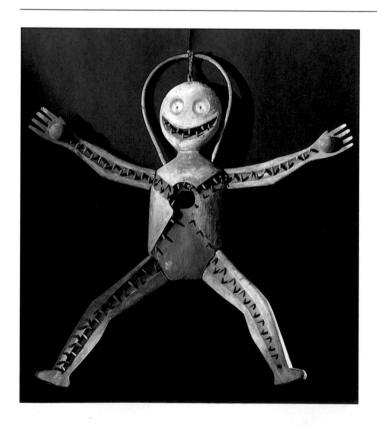

AMULETS were a vitally important part of life. They could be anything from a feather to a tooth, and were either attached to clothing or used to decorate tools and weapons. Family charms were left around the house in special places. Sometimes the shaman suggested what charms a family should make. These ideas were passed down from generation to generation.

THERE WERE THREE MAIN SPIRITS, who between them controlled everything in the Eskimos' world. They were: the Spirit of the Air, who gave breath and was responsible for wind and weather; the **Spirit of the Sea** who controlled the souls of all sea creatures; and the **Spirit of the Moon**, who had influence over the souls of all land animals.

◁ *The shaman was believed to have the power to see into other peoples' bodies, as well as expose his own. This Alaskan skeleton model represents this power.*

NEWLY DEPARTED SOULS sometimes caused trouble among those left behind, unless care was taken to honour them. When a person died, their belongings, or replicas of them, were placed near the body, in order to please them. A woman would be buried with her needles, lamps and cooking pots; a man with his tools and weapons.

THE MAIN FESTIVAL SEASON ran from late November through to summer. The major festival was the Bladder Festival, in honour of the the seal, which was so important to the Eskimos' survival. The bladders of all the seals killed in that year were inflated and hung around the *kashim* where the men entertained the souls of the seals with songs and dances. Finally, the bladders were returned to the sea.

coat of an angakok – an Inuit shaman

stick or antler for banging the shaman's drum

hand symbols ward off evil spirits

◁ *This is the story of how this costume was designed: one day, a man who wanted to become a shaman went hunting and killed a caribou. The caribou turned into a pregnant woman, who died giving birth. Some other caribou turned into men, who told the hunter to return home and make a coat in the same design as the one worn by the woman. He did so, and that is how he became a shaman.*

Making contact

Up until the sixteenth century, arctic culture flourished without much interference from other peoples. Then, around 1550, European and Siberian explorers arrived, quickly followed by fur traders, whalers and missionaries. These people had a deep and lasting effect on the Eskimos' way of life.

CONTACT WITH PEOPLE from outside the Arctic brought with it many consequences – the most serious being disease. The Eskimos had never been exposed to diseases such as measles or flu and so had little or no resistance to them. Disease spread through the region, killing thousands of Eskimos in its wake.

EXPLORERS came in search of the Northwest Passage, a route across the top of Canada which would be a short cut for ships sailing from Europe to the Far East. Although relations between the explorers and the natives were usually friendly, some Eskimos were killed and a few were taken prisoner.

△ *This photo was taken in 1900 at Dawson in Alaska. The trapper has a sled full of caribou skins. Furs were in great demand then, but the trade collapsed in the 1940s.*

WHALERS followed in the footsteps of the explorers. The bowhead whale provided oil and whalebone for ladies' corsets. Many Eskimos worked as crew members and were paid with goods and food. But the whalers brought with them guns which changed the way Eskimos hunted. Huge numbers of animals were killed for the fur trade, reducing stocks so much that some Eskimos starved.

◁ *This store at Nome, Alaska, sold furs and artefacts. The Eskimos had to sell objects for cash in order to buy the American goods they had become dependent on.*

FUR TRADERS were attracted to the Arctic by its rich wildlife. The trappers were mostly native people. They were encouraged by the traders to bring in valuable beaver, wolf and fox furs, which were made into fashionable coats and hats. In exchange for the furs, the Eskimos received food, guns and ammunition. This meant that the Eskimos spent less time hunting for their own food, and that they came to rely on food and goods provided by the traders.

KEY FOR MAP SYMBOLS

- ✶ fur trappers
- ⚓ explorers
- ✝ missionaries
- 〜 whalers
- 🏠 settlers

△ *This map illustrates why Americans and Europeans ventured into the arctic region.*

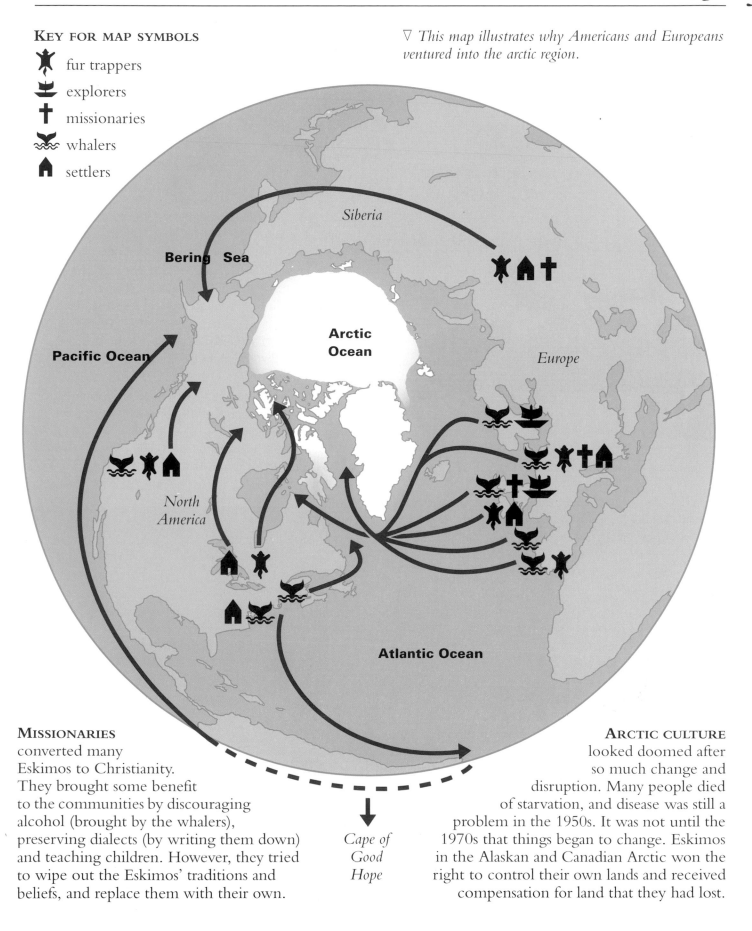

Siberia

Bering Sea

Pacific Ocean

Arctic Ocean

Europe

North America

Atlantic Ocean

Cape of Good Hope

MISSIONARIES
converted many Eskimos to Christianity. They brought some benefit to the communities by discouraging alcohol (brought by the whalers), preserving dialects (by writing them down) and teaching children. However, they tried to wipe out the Eskimos' traditions and beliefs, and replace them with their own.

ARCTIC CULTURE
looked doomed after so much change and disruption. Many people died of starvation, and disease was still a problem in the 1950s. It was not until the 1970s that things began to change. Eskimos in the Alaskan and Canadian Arctic won the right to control their own lands and received compensation for land that they had lost.

Between two worlds

Today, Eskimos have many of the conveniences of modern day life. They live in permanent homes with central heating and watch television. They use snowmobiles (skidoos) instead of sleds and dogs and regular air services connect them to the rest of the world. However, aspects of their lives are still very traditional. Living off the land is still very important and crafts such as sewing skins, carving and basket-making still thrive.

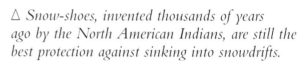

△ *Snow-shoes, invented thousands of years ago by the North American Indians, are still the best protection against sinking into snowdrifts.*

A SNOWMOBILE is a motorised version of the traditional sled. It is now the fastest way of travelling across the Arctic. A snowmobile owner needs to be an excellent mechanic: if his machine breaks down far from home, he could die unless he is able to repair it quickly. Arctic peoples rarely keep husky dogs now, except for tracking seal breathing holes, or for racing in dog-sled events.

KAYAKS are rarely seen in the Arctic today. However, they are now used in all parts of the world, mainly for sport and recreation.

△ *This Saami caribou herder takes a break during the spring move to summer pastures in northern Norway. Snowmobiles are very fast, reducing journey times from days to hours.*

THE ESKIMOS DESIGNED specialist equipment for the arctic environment that has never really been bettered. Their boats, clothes, tools and weapons form the basis of the most sophisticated cold-weather gear used by people in northern regions of the world today.

HARPOONS are still used to hunt sea mammals. These weapons have the same basic mechanism of a throwing stick with a detachable point, just as they had thousands of years ago. Modern skis have also remained true to their original design – long and slender with curved tips – which was based on wood or whalebone sled runners.

▷ *The work of Inuit soapstone carvers is very highly skilled and is in great demand from collectors, museums and art galleries. Both men and women carve, and by selling their art they can supplement their income. This man from Qeqertat in Greenland is carving out a figure from local stone.*

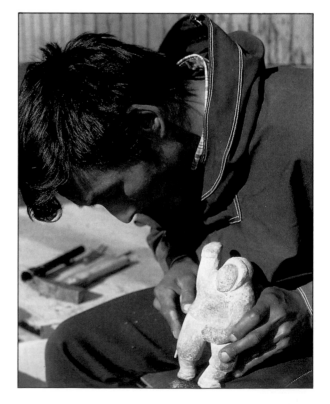

◁ *The parka is an original Eskimo design that is still the best way to keep warm in freezing weather.*

THE ART OF THE ARCTIC is alive and well. A whole new generation of modern artists is producing sculptures, baskets, drawings and prints in the traditional way. Some of the artefacts are sold to tourists, while other items are bought by collectors for very high prices, enabling small communities to earn a reasonable living.

FESTIVALS AND GAMES are keeping the stories, dances, songs and skills of the Arctic alive. Blanket toss, seal skinning and touchball are some of the activities that are still practised today.

IN THE PAST FORTY YEARS, the Eskimos have endured a complete upheaval in the way of life that served them so well for 3,000 years. However, such is the strength of their culture that many traditions have survived and are being rediscovered and taken up by today's generation.

THE PARKA is so successful a design that it has been copied around the world. Modern parkas are less bulky because of the use of man-made fabrics and fillings, but it is doubtful that they are as warm as the original garment. Today, although Eskimos wear shop-bought clothes, such as jeans and T-shirts, they still wrap up in sealskin or caribou trousers and a fur-trimmed parka in the winter or when hunting on the ice. Skins are still prepared in the traditional way by women.

HUNTERS are still greatly respected among arctic peoples – even though some of them now have jobs and can only hunt at the weekend. School holidays are timed to coincide with spring hunting or summer fishing, so the children can go camping with their parents and learn how to hunt in the traditional way.

▷ *This Inuit father and son wait patiently by a breathing hole in late spring. It is important to the Inuit that their children learn how to hunt and fish.*

Glossary

Aleut A western Arctic people from the Aleutian Islands, off the west coast of Alaska. Aleut is also one of the main languages spoken in the Arctic.

amulet A carving or object (anything from a stone to a bird's beak), that is kept as a magical charm. It can be worn, kept in the home or attached to tools or weapons, and is believed to protect its owner against evil or illness.

anthropologist A person who studies the culture, language and behaviour of people.

archaeologist A person who studies the remains of buildings and artefacts from the past.

Arctic The area of land within the Arctic Circle, around the North Pole. It includes parts of North America, Europe and Asia. It is almost permanently cold, but much of the Arctic is free of snow in July and August.

artefact A man-made object.

baleen A hair-like material that forms long plates in the mouths of some whales, such as the bowhead. These whales have no teeth, but use the baleen to sieve plankton out of seawater.

blubber The fat of whales, seals and other marine mammals. It can be eaten, or melted to make oil for light or to make an ointment.

bolas A hunting weapon that consists of between four and eight ivory weights attached to an equal number of strings. It is flung into the air to knock birds out of the sky.

bow-drill A simple drill made from a flint or metal-tipped stick. A bow string is wrapped around the stick and pulled back and forth. This makes the stick turn, so the sharp end drills.

bowhead whale A baleen whale that feeds in the Arctic Ocean during the summer. Bowheads have large heads and curved jaws.

breathing hole As the sea freezes over, sea mammals maintain holes or cracks in the ice, so that they can come to the surface to breathe.

cache A hole, dug into the permafrost and lined with stones. It was used for storing meat in the Arctic.

caribou A large brown deer with long antlers which lives on the tundra in summer. In winter, caribou head south. They also inhabit many Canadian Arctic islands and parts of Greenland. In Europe, caribou are called reindeer.

crampon A spiked frame attached to a boot which makes it easier to grip the ice.

dialect A regional variety of a language. In the Arctic, there are many varieties of the three main languages.

Eskimo A term that may be used to mean all peoples of the Arctic.

freeze-up This refers to the time of year, usually around October, when temperatures fall in the Arctic and rivers and parts of the sea freeze solid.

harpoon A hunting weapon consisting of a detachable harpoon head and a line fixed to a long shaft.

Ice Age Throughout history there have been several ice ages – the world's climate became very cold and parts of Northern Europe, Asia and America were completely covered in ice. The last Ice Age lasted about 40,000 years and ended about 11,000 years ago.

ice floe A large sheet of floating ice that can be attached to land, or free-floating in the sea.

Inuit A people living throughout the Arctic. Different groups include the Copper Inuit, Caribou Inuit, Baffinland Inuit, Alaskan Inupiaq and West and East Greenland Inuit. Inuit is also the name of one of the three main language groups of the Arctic.

iglu-viga A dome-shaped snowhouse constructed from blocks of ice.

kayak A long, slim arctic canoe used for hunting in calm, coastal waters and in rivers.

labrets Plugs of ivory, stone or wood, that men wore in holes cut in their lower lip.

leister A three-pronged fishing spear.

polynya An area of sea that never freezes over, because it has such strong currents.

permafrost Ground that is permanently frozen. In the Arctic, the permafrost is on the surface of the ground, almost always covered by ice and snow. In the subarctic, permafrost lies deep under a layer of thawed earth.

shaman A man or woman with special powers who could influence good and bad spirits to solve problems within the community.

sinew A tough, fibrous tissue that joins muscle to bone.

snow knife A curved knife used for cutting blocks of wind-packed snow. The blocks are used for building shelters.

sod house A house dug into the ground and built with walls of sod, or turf.

Spirit of the Air The most powerful spirit in the Eskimo world. The Spirit of the Air had power over the whole world and all of nature.

Spirit of the Moon The spirit that controlled all land animals. It was particularly important to people who hunted caribou.

Spirit of the Sea The spirit that controlled all sea creatures.

subarctic The area of land just south of the Arctic Circle, including parts of Asia, North America and Europe. Winters are almost as cold as in the Arctic, but summers are warmer.

toboggan A flat piece of wood or skin, used for transporting goods across the ice.

tradebeads Glass beads offered by traders in exchange for Eskimo goods and services.

tree line The line beyond which it is too cold and windy for trees to grow.

tundra A cold, dry, treeless region stretching from the Arctic to the subarctic. For more than half the year, the tundra is covered in snow but in spring the ground is covered with flowers.

ulu A woman's knife, used to prepare animal hides before they are sewn together.

umiak A large open boat used for whaling and made from skins stretched over a wooden frame.

Yupik A people from Alaska in the western Arctic. There is also a smaller group of Yupik in Siberia. Yupik is one of the three main language groups of the Arctic.

yurt A Siberian dwelling which is usually a circular tent made of felt or reindeer hide.

Index